MASTERING THE ART OF MANAGING MONEY

MASTERING THE ART

OF MANAGING MONEY

Secrets for Success In the Management of Personal And Corporate Finances

SHAFII A. NDANUSA MBA, ACCA

This book was printed in the United States of America.

To order additional copies of this book, contact:
Xlibris Corporation
0-800-644-6988
www.xlibrispublishing.co.uk
Orders@xlibrispublishing.co.uk
302907

CONTENTS

PART ONE
BACKGROUND LESSONS

PART TWO
STEPS TO MASTERY OF THE ART

The Knowing Phase

Without an understanding of the basic principles and concepts of financial education, it is practically impossible to be successful in the management of financial resources.

The Planning Phase

Vision makes the whole difference between the blind and the seeing. The measure of success in the management of money is attributable to the determination of specific financial objectives. Vision helps to define the goal, the roadmap and the targets to be achieved.

The Strategic Assessment Phase

Dealing with competing needs in the context of limited resources can only be effectively tackled through justification and prioritization. This step ensures that the so-called unlimited wants do not become a constraint to success in the management of finances.

The Action Phase

This is the active engagement phase of managing money. It is the stage at which strategy is expressed by action and where action also informs/

impacts on strategy. A financial code of conduct is proposed for all so that individuals may act following a set of guiding principles or rules.

The Choice Phase

Regardless of the outcome of a financial decision, it is vital that the lesson inherent in an experience is not lost as this is vital to future financial strategy development. The more people learn from their failures, the less likely they will fail again.

Contentment is a choice and not a product of personal financial decision making. Individuals must understand that this choice is available to all and also have the courage to choose to have it. Contentment has a positive effect on future financial decision making for the decision maker.

DEDICATION

To the hundreds of millions of humanity

Who struggle financially on a daily basis . . . .

ACKNOWLEDGEMENTS

Writing a book meant for general use is certainly not an easy task. Apart from the author, many other unseen hands contribute to the project. Some people do this knowingly, while others make their contributions without knowing that they are in fact part of a worthy cause. I am convinced that days, weeks, months and years of study and research have not been in vain. I am also convinced that the daily interactions I have had with a wide range of people over time prepared me for this project. To all those who have been part and parcel of this book, whether knowingly or unknowingly, I am thankful.

A very special thank you goes to the members of my family. I must thank my wife, who provided me with the freedom of time and space to clearly articulate my thoughts for this book. I must also thank my daughter, who loaned me some time off from the daily family time to conclude this work. Without their support, this book would remain in my archives as part of my unpublished works.

I would also like to thank the so many authors, teachers and co-students whom over the years have taught me valuable lessons about money, education, life and living. These tutors and colleagues of mine are too numerous to mention. As an unrepentant student of finance, economics, history and leadership strategy, I am still deeply engrossed in learning from my many teachers and colleagues. And once again I remain grateful.

INTRODUCTION

As a finance professional writing a book on the art of money management, I faced a dilemma from the onset. My goal was to write a book that will be very simple and easy to appreciate by a wide spectrum of readers, regardless of whether they had any previous knowledge of financial principles or not. Having acquired extensive technical and practical training on money management matters, I found it quite challenging translating the sophisticated finance concepts that we use on a daily basis to simple language.

The dilemma was compounded when I came to realize that the subject matter (the art of managing money) is not well covered by currently existing books and finance literature. Most of the existing literature on the management of finances approached the subject matter from the technical or scientific points of view. This left me with just one key category of references to learn from; the very wide and varied experiences of people who have been financially successful from all walks of life.

In addition to the above and because of the practical nature of the subject matter, it is natural that the content of the book is laced with some motivational flavor. I must restate that the challenge of simplifying some sophisticated money management concepts is one I faced throughout the course of writing this book.

The resulting consequence is that this is not a traditional finance book. It is the result of an attempt to simplify a subject matter that is quite very dear to all and yet quite poorly understood by most. While I agree with most people that traditional financial management literature may be sophisticated and sometimes complex. I do not hold the view that learning about the management of finances is a boring subject matter.

If money management is dear to all of us, then we must not consider learning how to master it a boring subject matter. In fact, we should approach it with the highest sense of seriousness and responsibility. We must remove any barrier that impedes our understanding of this very delicate and useful subject matter. It is in view of this clear and present challenge that I took up the task of coming up with this book. An approach is made to present money management from the individual and corporate point of view and to use language that is easy to appreciate.

The science of financial management is a well established field of finance with simple as well as sophisticated theories to support a vast array of principles and practices. Despite the advancements in theoretical financial management, nation states, companies and individuals are still facing difficult financial times. Business failures and bankruptcies are common phenomena. This occurs at different levels, from the individual to the corporate as well as societal.

The traditional financial management literature appears to be too technical and theoretical in nature thereby failing to meet the needs of most individuals who seek further knowledge on this subject matter. As humans, we are emotional by nature and these emotions come out strongly in matters that have to do with money. Personal financial management presents a lot of people with a dilemma and this is because too much theory has been built around the subject matter.

Just the way I believe in the science of financial management, I also believe that there is an art to it particularly when one desires to succeed in the management of personal finances. We are most often quick to lampoon corporate managers when businesses fail, but should a similar assessment be made of the management of our own personal finances, it is highly unlikely that very many of us will pass this litmus test.

It is in view of the dearth of literature on the art of managing money that I have decided to come forth with this simple, easy-to-use book. It is a distilled summary of various lessons I have learnt over the years both from the science and the art of financial management. Sometimes there is this central focus on the individual. This was designed to give the book that human touch that is so desperately required in these times of great economic uncertainty.

The lessons inherent are timeless and relevant regardless of climes. It does not matter whether the individual, the corporate entity or the economy is emerging from a recession or in the deep throes of one, the principles are timeless. It also does not matter whether the individual, company or society concerned in financially bankrupt—the steps once diligently followed would result in a better experience for all stakeholders from financial decision making.

Mastering the Art of Managing Money is applicable not just at the individual level, but also at the corporate as well societal levels. The focus on the individual was designed simply to personalize the lessons but it applications transcends the individual. It is widely held that once appropriate training is delivered at the individual level, it is much easier for the same lessons to be transmitted to the wider corporate community and subsequently at the societal level. This book assumes that the individual lies at the heart of all societal development efforts.

Modern man attaches so much importance to money matters such that many are of the view that money or its lack is the source of all evil. This situation is not made easy by the confusing role money sometime plays in the lives of people. The management of personal finances has thus become a great area of perennial human concern for all people in all cultures and societies.

Despite the fact that the theory of financial management is well chronicled in contemporary books, the art of financial management that is responsible for the practical success is less covered. The confusion is made worse when those who are appropriately schooled in the science of financial management still fail in the art thereby raising more questions.

I believe in the law of process. And I am convinced that the recommended steps once diligently followed will result in a more positive experience for anyone involved in taking financial decisions. The book is designed to reduce the incidence of buyer's remorse and all the other negative feelings that come after taking financial decisions. In fact it is proposed that in life, one should actually look forward to each opportunity for taking financial decisions. This is because each financial decision an individual takes add to his experience. And this experience will ensure that past mistakes from financial decision making are not repeated in the future.

This suggests that ongoing learning is an important aspect of financial education. It might be necessary to first of all learn about a new way of doing business or investment, unlearn some of the earlier lessons learnt and then relearn new ways of making the business or investment better. To be successful in the managing finances either from the individual or corporate point of view, the following five phases of activity is recommended:

1. Phase One: Acquire Financial Education
2. Phase Two: Clearly define your Financial Vision, Objectives and Budget
3. Phase Three: Justify and Prioritize your Expenditures
4. Phase Four: Develop/Adopt a Financial Code of Conduct
5. Phase Five: Always Learn and Choose Contentment

An attempt is made here to present money management not in the manner of a rocket science or a field with so much mathematical jargon but as something that as simple and as basic as human nature. An attempt is also made to show that every person who is involved in making one financial decision or another can experience beneficial outcomes from such decisions. This positive experience is possible regardless of whether specific monetary targets are achieved or not.

PART ONE

BACKGROUND LESSONS

CHAPTER ONE

WHAT MANAGING MONEY IS ALL ABOUT

Why You Need to Manage Your Finances?

One of the greatest challenges facing mankind today is management of financial resources. Every single day of our lives, we are confronted with innumerable examples of why we need to take control of this very important aspect of our lives. In all societies, the financial bankruptcy of an individual or a business in not new. But today, there is an emerging trend that is not only disturbing but equally dangerous. This is the threat of financial bankruptcy hanging over sovereign nations or put simply civilized societies. The invention of money as a means of exchange in the modern world has drastically affected the world in which individuals and societies relate in the contemporary world.

Kindly go through the following list and then try to identify one person that does not have money concerns?

1. The Poor
2. The Rich
3. The Young
4. The Old
5. The Literate
6. The Illiterate
7. The High in Society
8. The Low in Society

9. The Men
10. The Women
11. The Black
12. The White
13. The Student
14. The Teacher
15. The Manager
16. The Subordinate
17. The Mayor
18. The Governor
19. The Prime Minister
20. The President

You will agree with me that regardless of whom you are or your status in society, we all have serious concerns over the management of money. The sad truth is that managing money is not as difficult as it is made to seem. It is a skill that can be learned through the application of sound money management principles in the daily transactions of everyday life.

The poor must manage money properly in order to get by and also escape from the shackles of poverty. The rich must also be concerned about maintaining the value of the money they have as well as growing it.

The young must plan properly for future financial responsibilities. Being young presupposes that one has so much energy and time to be actively engaged in work. However, because over time responsibilities grow for the young, there is thus the need to prepare adequately for the financial needs of the future. The old are concerned about maintaining health and financial stability. This requires attention to be paid to money matters too.

Men and women equally have needs for finances. As human beings with personal dreams and aspirations, they strive to fulfill the attainment of their goals by properly managing the resources at their disposal such as time and money.

The manager of a company must properly manage its financial resources so that employees can be paid as at when due. The manager must also ensure that the company has a steady cash flow that will guarantee the settlement of routine financial obligations over time.

Political leaders such as Mayors, Governors and Presidents also have serious concerns about money matters. Financial resources are required to pay public servants, members of the national security services as well as the provision of critical economic infrastructure. This is in addition to many other compelling needs of the society that requires the application of money.

Both from the personal and corporate point of view, the management of money cannot be treated with kid gloves. It is vital to healthy living in the way that air is required for breathing. When an individual is financially bankrupt, it is easy to see how this would impact on his credibility, assets base and credit worthiness. When a company is also financially bankrupt, it is equally easy to predict that the company may eventually cease to exist. But when a society or sovereign nation is financially bankrupt with so much debt, there is actually no limit to the imagination of how that will affect that same society and many other connected societies too. This is what the danger of the looming sovereign debt crisis of Europe and North America poses to the entire world economy.

The modern economy of all nations is entirely dependent on the sound health of the financial system. Should the health of any financial system in any country be compromised, there is the tendency that it will impact of the overall health of the global financial community. What the world is facing today in terms of the looming sovereign debt crisis is unprecedented. Who will pay the price for the failure of a society's financial system? Sovereign nations have accumulated so much debt to the point whereby meeting up to their repayment obligations is practically impossible without a default.

From the personal point of view, a student who spends his entire pocket money in purchasing clothes for instance will face a challenge when an important need like the need for food crops up. This is a very simple yet common money mismanagement practice amongst college students who are just beginning to learn how to manage their personal finances. It is a familiar classic case of diverting short term funds (pocket money) to long term use (clothing). The net effect of this scenario is that cash will not be available when it is needed.

One of the key causes of business failure is the poor management of finances. A company that does not take into careful when and how to dispense of its financial resources is doomed to face liquidity problems. Liquidity problems arise when a company has financial obligations that have crystallized and yet lacks the cash to offset those obligations. For instance, when funds meant for the payment of wages and salaries are used to purchase additional plant and equipment. Employee salaries thus cannot be paid as at when due and this could spark off a labor crisis that may lead to the eventual shut down of operations.

In addition to the above, when the flow of cash in and out of a corporate entity is not properly managed, there is a tendency that when it time to pay back obligations such as debt there will be a default.

The same situation as outlined above applies to any society or community that is regarded as a corporate or sovereign entity. The problem associated with mismanagement of finances is compounded for a sovereign entity because in addition to providing some services purely on commercial terms, the sovereign nation also provides certain social services. With the sovereign entity such as a nation, there is this assumption of a healthy financial system to support economic activities. When the financial system collapses, confidence in the payments mechanism is eroded. The value of the country's currency is impacted. Inflation, interest rates and many other factors may come in to create further problems for a sovereign entity that is already struggling to cope with the loss of confidence in its economic system.

Purposes for Managing Money

Individuals usually strive to manage their finances for the following purposes:

1. To provide adequately for routine consumption needs.
2. To save a portion of earnings for the rainy day.
3. To provide for worthwhile investment purposes.
4. To purchase assets required for personal use.
5. To purchase assets required for business use.
6. To provide funds for meeting past and current liabilities.
7. To put some funds aside for the meeting of financial emergencies.
8. To consistently build a personal assets base so as to promote economic growth and development.

Companies seek to manage their finances for the following purposes:

1. To raise funds for investments in viable business proposals.
2. To raise funds for the payment of staff salaries and wages.
3. To raise the funds for financing capital assets acquisitions.
4. To raise funds for investing in working capital needs.
5. To raise funds required for the payment of administrative and operational expenses.
6. To raise funds for offsetting current and long term liabilities.
7. To raise funds required to offset tax liabilities to the tax authorities.
8. To raise funds required for paying dividends to share holders. Dividend payments to shareholders represent an aspect of the return on investment. If a company has a regular dividend payment policy in

place, part of the reasons it manages its finances is to enable it honor this very important obligation to shareholders when the need arises.

A sovereign entity such as a nation state seeks to manage its financial resources for the following purposes:

1. To provide funds required to meet the requirements for the provision of basic social infrastructure such as water, basic health, sanitation and welfare needs.
2. To provide funds required to meet expenditure on the security. Internal security and protection from external aggression is a key feature of all sovereign entities. The funding of these activities places heavy a financial burden on sovereign nations.
3. To invest in key areas of the economy that are usually capital intensive and not favored by the private sector.
4. To develop human capacity required to meet present and future economic manpower needs.
5. To provide funds for investment in the provision of basic economic infrastructure. The provision of basic economic infrastructure contributes to creating an enabling environment for private sector investments to thrive.
6. To provide incentives for different aspects of the economy where participation is being encouraged.
7. To raise finances through taxation and other means required to meet the country's economic goals and targets.
8. To improve the value of the country's currency, trade and economy.

From the general perspective it is clear that the managing finance is all about the following four elements:

Element 1: The objectives of financing.

Element 2: Securing the financing.

Element 3: Allocating/Using the financing.

Element 4: Controlling the financing to ensure it is in line with the objectives.

CHAPTER TWO

WHY THE SCIENCE OF FINANCIAL MANAGEMENT IS SIMPLY NOT ENOUGH?

The Science of Managing Money/Finances

I want to begin this chapter with a short and simple exercise. After going through the list below, I want to suggest that you take note of how many of the concepts you are thoroughly familiar with. Take note of the phrase; THOROUGHLY FAMILIAR:

1. Cost Concept
2. Revenue Accounting
3. Maximization of Profits
4. Minimization of Cost
5. Financial Accounting
6. Management Accounting
7. Loan Syndication
8. Earnings Per Share
9. Financial Strategy
10. Dividend Yield
11. Capital Growth
12. Gearing
13. Bankruptcy and Liquidation
14. Share Price
15. Market Capitalization
16. Corporation Tax Liability

17. Contingent Liability
18. Risk and Return
19. Liquidity and Profitability
20. Value Added Tax
21. Value for Money
22. Money and Capital Markets
23. The Stock Market
24. Fundamental Analysis
25. Inflation and Asset Values
26. Consolidation
27. Annual Reports and Accounts
28. Deferred Income
29. Deferred Tax
30. Discounted Cash Flow
31. Capital Budgeting
32. Capital Investment Appraisal
33. Capital Asset Pricing Model
34. Free Cash Flow
35. Options, Future and Swaps
36. Fixed Income Securities
37. Internal Rate of Return
38. Cost of Equity Capital
39. Mix and Yield Variances
40. Zero-based Budgeting
41. Net Present Value
42. Dividend Valuation Model
43. Invoice Discounting
44. Cash Operating Cycle
45. Creative Accounting
46. Mergers and Acquisitions
47. Hostile Takeovers
48. Good Housekeeping
49. Hedging
50. Efficient Markets Hypothesis

While it is likely that we may have heard about some or most of the financial concepts listed above, it is quite likely that most of us are only thoroughly familiar with a very few of them. This is the problem with the field of finance. It is so wide with so many areas of specialization, each area with a distinct vocabulary of its own. This therefore presents a formidable challenge to a lot of people who just crave for familiarity with this all important yet strange field of human endeavor. Note that the above list of financial concepts is just a tip of the iceberg. There are actually many more.

The seeming endlessness of theoretical financial concepts is one of the reasons that discourage learning in this subject area. As you become familiar with one area such as taxation, you begin to come across more advanced concepts even within the taxation discipline. So the learning appears to never end. This situation coupled with the fact that theoretical finance literature have been presented in a sophisticated manner over the years have led to a situation of poor understanding of the subject matter.

My message at this juncture is simple and is that; from the practical point of view having knowledge of the science of financial management is simply not sufficient to guarantee success in the practical management of finances. In fact, it is grossly misleading to assume that because you have acquired so much book knowledge in the field of managing finances such that you will be a natural practical act of the management of finances. It is equally not being suggested that you must acquire all the technical book knowledge on financial management before you master the art of managing finances.

The Art of Managing Money/Finances

Mastering the art of managing money is an entirely different ball game. It goes beyond the mere acquisition of a wide variety of book knowledge to taking concrete steps that will guarantee success from the practical experience. An individual must be armed with a good understanding of the key finance concepts that are relevant to the art. An individual must also plan adequately for the any major financial undertaking using the basic and simple tools of planning available. In addition, the individual must maintain the right mental attitude to the management of personal as well as corporate finances and clearly understand the role of emotions in the process of financial decision making. Lastly, an individual must have the wisdom to see the lessons inherent in each financial experience and choose the emotional state of contentment following each experience.

In summary, recall the following:

1. That the theory of managing finances is usually too broad and sophisticated for the lay man to understand.

2. That the complexity of the theories of financial management creates a great deal of confusion for most non-finance people who decide to acquaint themselves with knowledge of the discipline.

3. That most of the existing traditional finance literature has not helped to further understanding as their presentations are usually done from the technical point of view. This presentation usually assumes that readers have knowledge of certain preliminary concepts of finance. In reality, this is not always the case.

4. That despite the endless list of theoretical finance concepts, it is not important to be familiar with all these concepts before one can succeed in the practical management of finances.

5. That mastering the art of managing finances requires much more than technical knowledge. It is actually a combination of the key elements of knowledge, vision and strength of character that is applied on a consistent and focused manner.

6. That anyone regardless of age, sex, social status, financial status, literacy level or geographical location can achieve mastering in the art of managing finances.

CHAPTER THREE

The Role of Emotions in the Management of Personal and Corporate Finances

Emotions are part of human nature. It is normal to have intense feelings of varying shades and colors from time to time. As human beings, it is impossible to exist in the world without feeling a spectrum of emotions within a single day. But the question is do we really know how our emotions affect our thoughts and actions? If we are adequately armed with this piece of information, it will make it easier for us to manage our emotions and thus our thoughts and actions.

Emotions are simply strong shades of feelings that overcome people from time to time. Some of the emotions are negative and constraining while others are positive and empowering. There are currently over three thousand (3,000) shades of emotions that are described by so many words. However, an individual only feels an average of a dozen of such emotions within a week.

Some positive and empowering emotions that lots of people are familiar with include the following:

1. Contentment
2. Happiness
3. Joy
4. Love
5. Encouragement
6. Freedom

7. Excitement
8. Motivation
9. Confidence
10. Enthusiasm
11. Goodness
12. Stimulation
13. Relief
14. Security
15. Satisfaction

Some negative and disempowering emotions that a lot of people are familiar with also include the following:

1. Fear
2. Anger
3. Guilt
4. Doubt
5. Worry
6. Anxiety
7. Resentment
8. Hate
9. Depression
10. Disappointment
11. Frustration
12. Humiliation
13. Hurt
14. Jealousy
15. Confusion
16. Insecurity
17. Boredom
18. Misery
19. Rejection
20. Overwhelmed

Beware of the Negative Emotions

A lot of research has been carried out on the way emotions affect human thought and consequently actions. The classification of emotions into negative and positive is a simple acknowledgement of the way and manner in which they affect human thoughts and actions. By implication, if negative emotions are not properly managed they have the tendency to result in negative consequences. The goal of managing negative emotions is to minimize its impact or eliminate completely. As human beings, we cannot avoid feeling negative emotions. But we must recognize quickly we they come up and manage them appropriately to curtail the damage they can do to our persons and interest.

Managing finances is about handling money. For individuals, companies and communities money issues can sometimes be very emotive. People that are involved in taking financial decision very often sacrifice reason for emotion. When financial decisions are taken purely on emotional grounds, there tendency for poor decisions are high. It is thus considered wise to approach financial decision making from the rational point of view rather than the emotional.

Our common humanity means that whether we like it or not, we must experience negative emotions. But what we do with the emotions is perfectly up to us. This is where we must have the awareness and wisdom to work on our negative emotions so as to eliminate or minimize their effect all together.

FEAR: The Biggest Emotional Threat to Success in Money Management

By far the biggest emotional threat to the achievement of success in the management of finances is the negative emotion of fear. Fear is an unpleasing sensation caused as a result of a feeling of closeness to danger or pain. When you are afraid of something, you are deterred from that thing.

Mastering the art of managing finances requires that the individual acquires valuable experience in financial decision making. With respect to the acquisition of financial experience, fear can act as a deterrent or a pushing force. For instance, fear of loss of investment can deter an individual from taking advantage of viable investment opportunities in an environment. Likewise, fear of poverty can push an individual to be aggressive about making financial investments in an environment. So everything eventually depends on the individual's attitude to the management of the emotion of fear.

Fear as a De-motivating factor

George Mason was raised by his parents in Midrand, South Africa. At the age of sixteen his father retired from the South African National Health Service where he had worked for the last thirty years of his life. Both parents were approaching the age of seventy at the time of retirement. The family income had been well planned over the years. A lot of savings was made to cater for future needs when both parents would have retired from active service. Shortly after the father's retirement, the family made a huge investment in the South African mining industry. The family's retirement savings was used up in addition to a business loan from the National Bank for Industrial Development. Despite the viable nature of the mining industry at the time of investment, unforeseen factors affected the demand for the products of the business. Five years after the commencement of operations, the company was still not profitable and the future prospects did not seem bright. Eventually the mining business had to be closed with significant loss of investment to the family. The family never recovered fully from this experience. George Mason became an individual who is fearful of loss of investment to the point that throughout his adult life, he refused to take advantage of profitable business opportunities. As a risk avoider, he had all his savings put in secured low yield government bonds rather than investing in high yield business start-ups.

Fear as a Motivating Factor

Frank Chilungu was born in a village 20 miles north of the Kampala. His parents were peasant farmers who depended heavily on land and the mercy of weather for survival. Frank was the eight child of the family. None of his elder one had gone to high school. Four of his elder siblings work with the parents on the family farm. Three others had left for the city of Kampala to do menial jobs. Frank was the first member of his family to attend High School located in a nearby community. At the age of fourteen, he was withdrawn from the school because the parents could not afford to pay the school fees. Frank had never been satisfied with the quality of life his family was living at the village. Having learnt to read and write. He has read of the wonderful life that is possible with the help of education. He made up his mind that he would not be deterred by the obstacles in his path. And that he will work very hard to live a life that is active and successful in every sense of the world. His fear of poverty pushed him to leave for the city at a tender age. For ten years, he did odd jobs and saved until he had enough money to enroll for adult classes. After his high school education, he won a scholarship to study computer science at the National University. He graduated top of his class and has moved on to achieve other successes. Mr. Frank Chilungu recently won the West Africa Young Entrepreneur of the Year Award with a cash prize of one million USD. He is an IT Entrepreneur with an established chain of companies providing website designs, software development and networking solutions with the West Africa sub region.

The above illustration of George Mason shows how the emotion of fear can make an individual avoid risk taking. And once an individual avoids taking financial decision, he loses out on worthwhile experience. Fear does not only deny you the chance of taking advantage of worthwhile investment opportunities, it denies you the opportunity of learning from the experiences you could have acquired.

In the case of Frank Chilungu, his morbid fear of poverty has propelled him to be bold and aggressive. Fear in this instance became the driving force behind effort required for achievement.

To master the art of managing finances, you must master your fears. In essence each time you are faced with a touch of fear in regards to the management of finances, take note of the following:

1. What am I really afraid of? Is it the fear of loss of money? Is it the fear of financial failure? Is the fear as a result of lack of knowledge about a specific course of financial action?
2. What is the responsible for this feeling? Any past historical lesson to be learnt from this?
3. How do I mitigate against this fear or risks?
4. What measures do I put in place to minimize the risks associated with the fear?
5. What lessons do I stand to learn from this particular experience?

CHAPTER FOUR

CONCEPTS OF SUCCESS

What does success mean to you as an individual?

What does success mean to your company?

What does success mean to your community?

What does success mean to your country?

These are questions that are bound to elicit a wide range of answers from a lot of people. It is in fact difficult to have a common meaning of what success is as each individual will only look at success from his own lens.

Generally, success may be defined as any or all of the following:

1. As the achievement of one aims
2. As the achievement of fame
3. As the achievement of wealth
4. As the achievement of position.

The above definitions of success are simple and basic and applicable to a wide range of situations. However, what is central to all the definitions is that success by nature is relative. It depends on the intention of the seeker of the success and the outcome that is actually sought. So it is not possible to have success in isolation.

What is Success in the Management of Money/Finances?

The easiest response is to assume that the third definition of success which equates it to the achievement of wealth represents success in the management of finances. However, this could be misleading because the definition itself is still a general one. If for instance, an individual views the attainment of position as the source of fame and wealth, it therefore means success to this individual will be defined by the achievement of position. For another individual who sees the achievement of a particular aim (such as graduating as an engineer) as the source of position, wealth and fame. Then to this individual, the achievement of this personal aim will represent success.

You need to be very clear what your definition of success is. You need to also be very how the attainment of the success connects to other aspects of your goals and desires. While the definition of success is personal to each individual or interested party, it is good practice to note the following about the above general definitions of success given above:

1. The first definition focuses on attainment of the individuals' aims. It is thus personal and unique to the individual. An athlete who aims to win the gold medal in the Olympics will consider himself as being successful once he achieves this goal.
2. The second definition looks at success as the achievement of fame. This definition is personal as well as relative in the sense that what sort of fame are we actually looking at? The definition depends on the manner and extent of recognition that is received from the society.
3. The third definition looks at success as the achievement of wealth. Unfortunately, this is the most common view of success held by a lot of people. Success in personal as well as relative using this definition. This is because there are differences as to what is regarded as wealth by different people. While one person may define success as the accumulation of say cash in the sum

of 1 million US Dollars, another may regard success as the accumulation of real estate property that is worth over 100 million US Dollars in market value.

4. The third definition looks at success as the achievement of a position of authority in society. This is another definition that equally personal as well as relative. For instance, an individual may consider himself to be successful the moment he is elected as the Mayor of his local city council. Another individual in the same community aspires to the position of President. Until this individual gets elected to the Presidency, he does not consider himself successful.

5. The notion of success that considers the achievement of all the above four definitions is the most holistic. It is comprehensive and goes beyond fame, wealth and position to the specific emotional needs of the individual. This suggests that true success is hinged on both external and internal factors. The external factors are those factors that are outside the individual such as fame, wealth and position. The internal factors are those factors that are within and unique to the individual such as happiness, joy and liberty.

Success as the Result of Thought and Action

The twenty first century is a period of remarkable change in technology. Significant scientific discoveries and advancements of the twentieth century prepared the ground for this rapid change. The world has truly become a global economy. The internet and other forms of information communications technologies have broken down the traditional barriers to knowledge acquisition/sharing, trade and distance. More than ever before, more people now have access to the tools that are capable of being used to transform their lives and experiences. But this personal and societal transformation begins first with a keen awareness of the possibilities inherent in the environment.

With an awareness of what is achievable then action is required in order to bring the realization of the goals to reality. A combination of thought and action is therefore the key to success in any undertaking. Whether an individual desires wealth, fame, position, health or contentment the same principle applies. In each circumstance you must have a mental awareness of the tools available for facilitating success. Thereafter, consistent and focused action is required to achieve the desired goals.

If you desire to succeed in the practical management of money, you must know that it is achievable. You must understand that the combination of your thoughts and action is what gives the result of success or failure. But before then you must clearly define your own personal definition of success in the management of money.

CONTENTMENT: The Only True Success

Contentment is an emotional feeling that refers to inner peace of mind or tranquility. It is a deep state of emotional satisfaction that is a key ingredient for healthy living. Contentment is sometimes a product of self actualization. The satisfaction that comes with knowing that you have given your best shot for the achievement of a goal is invaluable.

Very often, contentment is the one emotional state that most people strive for throughout the course of life. It is a state of harmony and emotional balance with self and nature. Contentment promotes harmonious living and co-existence. It is only when one is at peace with the self that one can ensure that others are also at peace. You cannot give what you don't have. To give happiness to others, you must first of all make yourself happy.

In all the above definitions of success, I hold the view that your emotional destiny is actually your final destiny. It is of no use to have acquired so much wealth and yet lack happiness either in your relationships with other people or even in your relationship with yourself. Therefore, if the sound management of your finances does not result in emotional contentment or happiness, then perhaps you are yet to be successful in this art.

Contentment is central to healthy living. It is the emotional platform for all the positive emotions that are experienced by people. Contentment covers the positive emotions of happiness, joy, love, security, confidence, encouragement, satisfaction and to harmony with self and nature. Emotional contentment is therefore the only true success.

DIMENSIONS OF SUCCESS

In the recent past, so much has been written about the concept of success to the point that sometimes it is confusing to really discern what real success is. It appears that mankind strives on a daily basis in pursuit of success regardless of whether the notion of success is understood or not. With a good understanding of what success means to you, it is easier to appreciate whether you have achieved your goals or not.

It is widely held that the entire purpose of life is to achieve success in any or all of the following areas or dimensions of success. These dimensions of success represent every ideal that you may aspire to in your pursuit of happiness in life.

1. Pursuit of Contentment and Inner Peace and Harmony
2. Pursuit of Harmonious Relationships
3. Pursuit of Physical and Mental Health
4. Pursuit of Financial Freedom and Independence
5. Pursuit of a deeper awareness of Self and Others
6. Achievement of Noble Goals and Self Actualization
7. Feeling a sense of Personal Fulfillment

PART TWO

STEPS TO MASTERY OF THE ART

Figure 1: Steps to Mastering the Art of Money Management

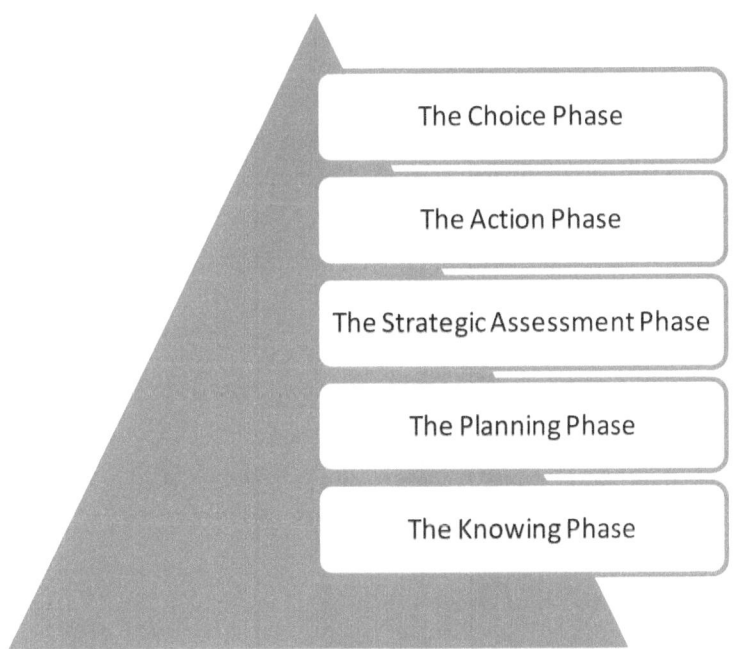

CHAPTER FIVE

Lesson One
Acquiring Financial Education

The Knowing Phase

Without an understanding of the basic principles and concepts of financial education, it is practically impossible to be successful in the management of financial resources.

What is financial education all about? Of what use is to me? Does it really matter whether I am financially literate or not? These are some of the questions that come to mind for most people. Some may further ask; must I go to school in order to learn the language of finance? What if I fail in the theory of this form of education? Can I still succeed in practice especially now that I seem to need success in this area so much? The list of questions is endless.

Financial education in this context is not about credit and debit entries or even about balancing complex books of accounts. But rather, it is simply about understanding the final effect that a financial decision has on your overall Net Worth. Put simply, does the decision add to my Net Worth or does it reduce my Net Worth. Sometimes understanding this dynamic is referred to as basic financial wisdom.

The most important activities to master in the art of managing finance is to have a good grip of earnings and spending. The ultimate goal of managing money is to strike a healthy balance between earnings and spending. Apart from acquiring background knowledge about some basic financial concepts, a good starting point is to usually identify all the sources of earnings available and all the items of expenditure of the individual, company or society.

The Goal of Financial Management

Essentially the goals of financial management may be summarized under the following three functions:

1. The Raising of Financial Resources
2. The Allocation/Usage of Financial Resources
3. The Control of Financial Resources

However, the ultimate objective of financial management is to ensure the efficient utilization of financial resources for the achievement of predetermined objectives. This is true for individuals as well as companies and societies.

It is important to be aware of this ultimate objective because it underpins every other need that comes up in the process of decision making. The individual who desires to make better quality financial decisions must begin by arming himself with the basics of financial education.

To know here simply means to be aware, to have in ones memory and to be familiar with the basic concepts and language of financial education.

Figure 2: Knowledge is central to the entire process of mastering the art of money management.

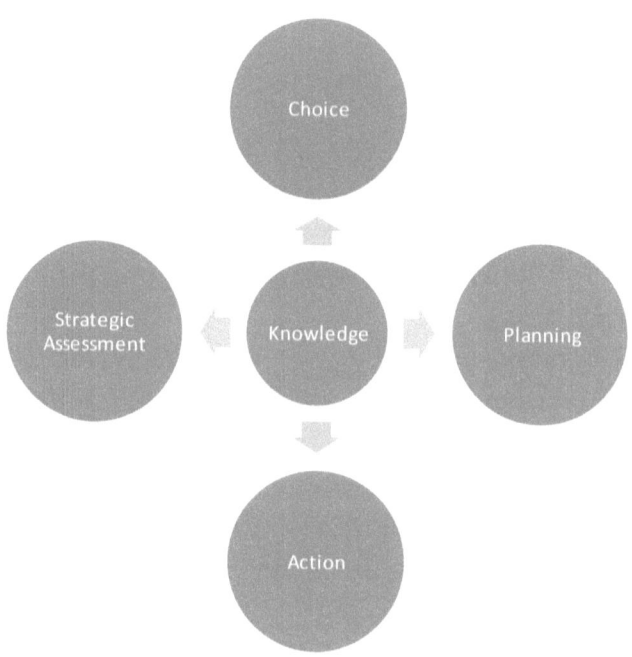

The Lesson

Knowledge is the pivot on which all thought is based. Knowledge informs and sharpens the thought process thereby helping to refine experience. The connection between thought and action in the successful management of financial resources is reinforced by the above diagram.

The importance of knowing cannot be overemphasized. Many writers and teachers have paid a lot of attention to this single element that is a key determinant of success in almost every human undertaking. It should not be surprising that this fundamental element is the first step in a series of steps required for success in the management of personal finances. It is however not an end in itself as knowledge is required to be continually honed by experience.

Raising of Financial Resources

An individual or a corporate entity that seeks to attain a certain financial or non-financial objective must first of all determine how to raise the financial resources required for the attainment of those objectives. Essentially, the choice of financing mode could come from equity or debt.

Equity refers to the direct personal contribution of the individual or corporate entity concerned to the requirements of the task at hand. This may be done through cash contribution or contributions in kind. It may be done using the combinations of both cash and kind. Equity therefore represents the ownership contribution to the total financial requirement for the attainment of a given objective.

For instance, Mr. Smith has decided to start a transport business requiring a total initial funding outlay of 20,000 US Dollars. The funding outlay is to cover for the cost of purchasing three used vehicles and some working capital to meet start up operation needs. From his personal savings and the personal assets owned by Mr. Smith, he decides to provide the three vehicles required as well as some cash for the start up working capital needs. The total monetary value of Mr. Smith's personal contribution to the transport business equals 20,000 USD. This sum represents his equity contribution to the business and in this instance is one hundred per cent (100%). The equity contribution was a combination of cash (working capital needs) and kind/assets (the three vehicles).

Assuming Mr. Smiths personal contribution to the business was just the three vehicles valued at 15,000 USD. He then approached a bank to borrow the balance of 5,000 USD required as start-up working capital needs for the business. The bank obliged his request and granted the business a loan in the amount of 5,000 USD. This sum of 5,000 USD represents debt capital to the business. The 15,000 USD then represents the equity capital. In this stance, owner's equity contribution is 75% of initial capital outlay while debt represents 25% of the initial capital outlay.

An individual must be clear about the project financing options available to him at the onset of each financial undertaking. Debt and equity have different features and each has its own separate cost implications. Availability or access to finance will determine whether a project or financial undertaking can be taken head on at least kept in view.

Allocating/Using Financial Resources

Because financial resources are relatively scarce, there must be used with a deep sense of responsibility. The efficient application of financial resources ensures that the most benefit is derived from their use. Often, there are always competing needs for financial resources. The ability to identify the most efficient financial asset allocation mix is a key attribute of successful financial management. The same rule applies whether an individual is allocating financial resources for meeting the family needs or the needs of the various project units/departments of a corporate organization.

In the context of investment decision making, an individual allocating financial resources must bear in mind the distribution of those resources between assets that are to held for long term purposes (referred to as fixed assets) and those assets that are to be held for short term purposes (referred to as current assets).

A note of warning, on no account should short term funds be used to finance long term assets. For instance, the monies meant for the payment of worker's monthly salaries and wages should never be used to pay for factory plant and equipments. This is a common mistake that creates liquidity (or cash) problems.

In the context of an individual managing family income, the same advice applies. On no account should monies meant for the purchase of food and groceries for the family's consumption be applied for the purchase of vehicles for the family.

Controlling Financial Resources

The control function works like a directing laser beam. The goal is to monitor the outcome of the application of financial resources and also ensure that they are making the maximum contribution to the attainment of predetermined objectives.

A simple monitoring and evaluation framework measures actual performance at each stage and then compares it to the target. Areas requiring improvements are taken care of to ensure that activities remain on track.

How Knowing contributes to Success in Personal Financial Management!

It is often said that knowledge is nothing without application. This means that the application of knowledge is what actually creates value for the knowledge itself. Well, if someone is unaware of the fact that the application of knowledge is what really unlocks potential, then there is more work to do.

Financial education aims to promote a general understanding as well as familiarity with the basic concepts and principles of financial management. The lessons are usually designed to ensure an acute awareness of financial issues on a consistent and long term basis. Most of all, financial education should be approached from the practical point of view and not from the technical/theoretical point of view.

Financial education is of use to everyone regardless of age, sex, clime, financial position or status in society. It is an issue that demands constant attention and care. More so in contemporary times, where a misleading basis of success is measured using the level of financial progress made by an individual, a company or a society.

You do not need to enroll in a formal school to receive financial education. Interestingly, observing the challenges on the streets of life provide some people with a good head start. But how many are lucky to have the vital lessons in this field of learning thrust at them at the early stages of life? How many more people still have the wisdom and strength of character to learn the proper lessons inherent in such early experiences?

Basic financial intelligence is not common. Because it is an uncommon skill a great deal of people struggle financially throughout life, even when all the tools to escape the proverbial 'rat race' are in their very hands.

If you fail in understanding the technical jargons of financial management, you can still make a success in the management of your personal finances. In my view, success in this area is more art than science. However, you must have a clear understanding of the principles guiding the foundations of financial wisdom. What I mean in effect is that you MUST understand the impact of each financial decision you take on your overall Net Value.

Consider yourself as a piece of stock in the market freely available for sale. Each financial decision you take impacts on your stock value. Your goal is to consistently increase your value hence you x-ray each decision on the basis of its impact on your stock value.

The Basics of Financial Education

If financial mastery is your goal, the very first step you need to take is to acquire some knowledge of the basics of financial education. This knowledge may be acquired informally or informally, on the street or at home, at work or at play, actively or passively. All around us, every minute of the day are events teaching us about how to take control of our financial destinies.

It is thus wise to use every opportunity available to us to gather more knowledge and experience on this delicate matter. No amount of training could ever be enough. We must endeavor to seek this form of education actively as well as passively. A day should not pass without new additions to our understanding and experience in respect of financial matters.

INCOME AND EXPENDITURE

In my opinion, the following are the two most important concepts for anyone who desires to succeed in the management of finances either at the individual or corporate level:

1. Income
2. Expenditure

Income in this context refers to the monetary amount(s), sum(s) or value(s) that you receive from employment, trade, business or vocation while expenditure refers to the amount(s), sum(s) or value(s) that you expend either on consumption or investment.

Income represents a financial inflow to your Net Worth while expenditure represents a financial outflow from your Net Worth. By extension, a financial savvy individual may view income as what he receives and see expenditure as what he gives out. Understanding the above analogy is vital as it determines your overall assessment of how a financial decision ultimately impacts on your Net Worth.

Simple Illustrations on Income

Illustration 1: Income from Employment—Salaries and Allowances

Richard Maxwell studied aeronautical engineering at the Middle East School of Aeronautics. He graduated in the year 2000 and is currently employed by Lufthansa Airlines. His present role includes the extensive reviews of the various aircraft models that the airline plans to introduce to the fleet. He earns an average monthly income of 10,000 USD representing salaries and allowances. His annual income of 120,000 USD thus represents his income from employment.

Illustration 2: Income from Trading

Mr. Lee owns a supermarket in downtown Shanghai. He stocks provisions and basic household items. Recently, he added small electronics to his stock list. He usually purchases his stock wholesale from the major suppliers. His supermarket is a retail outlet serving residents of downtown Shanghai. His average monthly turnover (or sales) is 200,000 USD. Of this sum, only ten per cent represents trading profits after the deduction of all the incidental expenses. The sum of 20,000 USD represents Mr. Lee's average monthly income from trading activity.

Illustration 3: Income from Ownership of Intellectual Property: Royalty

Mary Scott is an artist with a lot of graphic art works to her credit. In addition to attending at least three international art conferences every year, she hosts an exhibition of her own works at the annual New York Art Show. Ten of her works have been adopted by the cartoons section of

Universal Studios. These works feature in some cartoon films produced by Universal Studios. Mary Scott earns a fraction of the income that comes from the sales of these cartoon films by all the marketing outlets and agents of Universal Studios. In the last five years, Mary Scott's average annual royalty earnings from the sales by Universal Studios amount to 400,000 USD. The sum of 400,000 USD paid to her annually as royalty represents her income from ownership of intellectual property.

Illustration 4: Income from Ownership of Real Estate–Rental Income

Steve Trump is a major investment in the real estate market of Dubai. Over the years, he made significant investments in the residential estate development sector of the real estate industry of the city. An estate management firm coordinates and oversees the activities of all his investments within the city. It is estimated that on annual basis and from the residential estate development wing, he earns about 50 Million USD dollars as rental income. This sum represents Steve Trump's income from ownership of real estate in Dubai.

Illustration 5: Income from the Ownership of a Manufacturing Company

Global Steel Incorporated is a steel manufacturing corporation fully owned by James Burton. The company's largest production plant is based in Berlin and from there exports of steel products are moved and transported to various markets around the globe. Global Steel Incorporated maintains detailed books of accounts about all the financial transactions of the company. Every quarter a financial statement for the previous quarter of operation is submitted to James Burton who is the Chairman of the Board of Directors. Global Steel Incorporated has been profitable in the last 10 years of operation. The company has maintained a stable dividend payment policy over the last ten years. The average annual dividend payout for the last ten years stood at 10 Million USD per annum. This sum represents James Burton's income from the ownership interest held in the steel manufacturing company.

Illustration 6: Funds from Personal Debt Obligations

Abraham Newton is desirous of investing in a 2 Million USD business proposal for the construction and running of a medium-sized fruit processing plant to be located in Bradford. His total savings that is available for the project amounts to 1,700,000 USD. He is thus left with a shortfall of 300,000 USD. Having justified the business case for this business proposal, he approached the Midwest Bank for a loan. The bank agrees to provide the balance of 300,000 USD as a personal debt to Abraham Newton. The loan was secured with the London residence home of Abraham Newton as collateral. This sum of 300,000 USD represents a personal loan to Abraham Newton. In this instance, it does not matter if the loan is going to be used to fund a business proposal.

Illustration 7: Funds from Corporate/Business Debt Obligation

Going forward with example in illustration 6, assuming that Abraham Newton decides that he wants the business to bear the debt obligation. It therefore implies that the responsibility to pay back the loan will become a business obligation and thus not a personal obligation on Abraham Newton. In this instance, the proposed business must take on the status of a separate entity and thus be made liable to its debt obligation. The 300,000 USD loan may then be secured using some of the assets belonging to the business.

Importance of the above Illustrations

The purpose is the draw attention to the many sources of funding available to an individual or corporate entity. Owner's equity contribution to a business could come from income savings, assets and personal debt obligations. Business debt may also form a good source of finance where the need arises. The illustrations were designed to use simple everyday scenarios to identify the various sources of raising finance.

ASSETS AND LIABILITIES

Two equally important concepts of financial education are:

1. Assets
2. Liabilities

Robert Kiyosaki and Sharon Lechter in 'Rich Dad Poor Dad' attempted a basic definition of what an asset and liability is based on the effect it has on your Net Value. These definitions were simple and quite practical. The definitions actually proved that the practical meaning of the above concepts was different from the traditional textbook definitions of assets and liabilities. An asset was simply defined as something that puts money in your pocket while a liability was defined as something that takes money out of your pocket.

I agree that from the practical point of view, the above definitions are accurate and straight on point. Robert Kiyosaki and Sharon Lechter also held that most people in life fail financially because they spend their entire life buying liabilities instead of buying assets. And that financial struggle continues for most people in the real world because they lack the basic knowledge of the difference between a asset and liability. The above analogy justifies the importance of truly knowing what an asset and a liability is and from the practical point of view.

Assets may be regarded as property or rights acquisitions that have positive economic value while liabilities may be regarded as commitments that will need to be offset with some form of financial expenditure.

By extension, an individual may view an asset as an acquisition that has a far greater economic value than the cost of its acquisition in addition to the cost of its maintenance.

The defining feature of an asset in this context is that the present economic value of the asset outweighs the cost of its acquisition in addition to the cost of its maintenance. An asset is thus expected to fetch a higher monetary value through its usage and/or disposal.

In a similar vein, an individual may view a liability as an obligation that requires settlement at a financial cost. The obligation might be a historical obligation, a current obligation or a future obligation. Once the obligation crystallizes, it will need to be offset. The defining thread of a liability is that it is a commitment that requires offset with some form of expenditure.

From the above, it is easy to see that assets can be created in the process of some type of expenditure (such as investment expenditure) and liabilities can be incurred (or indirectly bought) in the process of generating income.

Illustrations on Assets and Liabilities

Illustration 8: Asset Acquired for Business Use

Bashar Abdallah works as a strategy consultant for over 10 construction firms based in Abu Dhabi. Over the years, there has been an increase in the demand for his strategy consulting services across the region. He now spends a significant amount of time travelling from one client's location to another trying to meet deadlines. Rather than to continue relying on public transport which is not always available when needed in odd hours, he decides to purchase a Toyota Land cruiser Jeep for his official movements. The vehicle was bought at the cost of 30,000 USD. This sum represents the cost of an asset that was acquired for business use.

Illustration 9: Asset acquired for Personal Use

Assuming that in the above example of illustration 8, Bashar Abdallah acquires a salon car for use after regular work hours. The expenditure of this vehicle will represent the cost of acquiring an asset for personal use. An asset acquired for personal can later be contributed into a business. At this time, the asset invariable becomes a property of the business.

Illustration 10: Liability Incurred on Consumption

Harriet Robinson works and lives in downtown Manhattan. Every weekend she visits the local grocery store on the main street to restock her grocery needs. The weekly purchases are usually charged to her credit card. These sums represent a form of liability that is incurred on consumption.

Illustration 11: Liability incurred on Investments

The Municipal Council Investment Authority of Nairobi Central has decided to invest in a tea making factory. Plants and equipments are to be imported from Australia. However, there is no local expertise within Kenya for the installation of the equipments. The cost of expatriate expertise for installation services was added to the cost of the investment proposal. It was agreed and included in the project contract between the equipment supplier and the Municipal Council Investment Authority that once equipments are supplied to the project site, full payment of the installation costs will be made to the equipment supplier. The cost of equipment installation represents a liability that is incurred in the course of investment.

To facilitate a deeper appreciation of the art of managing finances, the following tips are recommended as a general guide while dealing with the above concepts:

1. Earn as much income as is legitimately possible.
2. Save as most as possible from your free income earnings.

3. Look out for other funding options in the environment.
4. Spend as little as necessary on consumption expenditure.
5. Invest as much as is possible through investment expenditure.
6. Acquire assets that are economically safe and secured.
7. Continue to build you total assets column.
8. Be extremely cautious with liabilities.
9. Keep liabilities to the barest minimum.
10. Always review your financial performance in order to stay on track.

CATEGORIES OF EXPENDITURE

For the purposes of this book, I have classified expenditure into two categories:

1. Consumption Expenditure
2. Investment Expenditure

Consumption expenditure is expenditure on routine items that is required to meet the basic physiological needs of survival such as food, shelter, utilities and basic transport.

Investment expenditure is expenditure on assets or items with potentially higher economic outcomes. Expenditure on items like plants and equipment in a production factory represents this form of investment. Investment expenditure is also an indirect form of savings for future use.

The above classification is considered necessary due to the different ways in which each form of expenditure acts to affect the overall Net Worth of an individual or a corporate entity.

Illustrations on Expenditure

Illustration 12: Consumption Expenditure for a Manufacturing Business

A manufacturing company that pays its workers salaries and wages at a daily, weekly or monthly interval incurs other types of expenditure. Because labor is consumed in the manufacturing process, the cost of labor is represented by salaries and wages. This is thus a form of consumption expenditure for the manufacturing business.

Illustration 13: Investment Expenditure for a Real Estate Business

A real estate business that purchases land for real estate development is in effect making investment expenditure. The cost of the land, the estate plan, building materials, labor costs and other incidentals all form part to the investment expenditure. Eventually, all these costs will be pooled together to arrive at the total cost of the investment itself.

In the course of knowing, it would also do more good to get some basic understanding on some of the following issues:

1. What is the general economic environment like? Is the economy presently undergoing a recession or is it in a boom cycle?
2. With respect to the financial proposal at hand, what is the general business environment like for the area of interest? Is the industry profitable or do we have many failures in the industry?
3. What is the government's present fiscal policy stance on investments, the industry? Is the government promoting increased production and exports? Does the fiscal policy stance encourage new entrants into the industry?
4. What is the regulatory environment like for the industry? Is there free entry and exit into the industry? Is fair competition among industry players guaranteed?

5. What is the current tax regime in place? Are there clear tax rules and procedures? Is the tax authority business friendly? Is there multiple taxation going on? What is the available remedy to the challenges of multiple taxes? What are the specific tax rates for personal income tax, corporation tax, value added tax and other forms of taxes/charges.

6. What are the banking support services available in the environment? Is there easy access to credit for business finance?

7. What are the relevant laws in place guiding business activities? How do we ensure compliance with the laws and rules of business in the environment?

8. What will be our obligations in terms of corporate social responsibility?

CHAPTER SIX

Lesson Two
Defining The Financial Vision, Objectives And Budget

The Planning Phase

Vision makes the whole difference between the blind and the seeing. The measure of success in the management of money is attributable to the determination of specific financial objectives. Vision helps to define the goal, the roadmap and the targets to be achieved.

Financial Planning is designed to enable you envision your financial future and come up with realistic steps that will lead to the actualization of the vision. Clarity of vision is often the self distinguishing element between the blind and the seeing. Vision creates inspiration and idealism about the future. It is a dream of what an individual or organization or society intends to achieve well into the future. A clear financial vision of the future is a prerequisite for success in the management of finances. This does not only apply for the financial ambition, it applies to every other important aspect of life as well.

Imagine what it would be like to exist in the world as though one was blind? The thought is almost unbearable after one is accustomed to the benefits of seeing. Clarity of financial goals creates the semblance of sight from darkness. Unless one is very clear about his/her financial objectives, existence is merely in a state of financial blindness.

When you are blind financially, it is difficult to sense and see success even when it resides with you. It is equally impossible for one to anticipate and respond properly to all the factors that may affect the achievement of the desired financial goals.

Do you have a clearly defined vision of your financial objectives? Is the vision a definite state of being or a vague idea hanging somewhere in your head? Unless your responses to these questions are in the affirmative, then you have not started the journey to success in the management of finances.

The Objective of Financial Planning

Financial Planning is required by individuals, firms and societies in order to guarantee survival well into the future. For instance, a corporate entity operating without a financial plan is doomed to run into troubled waters. The same applies to the individual and the community. Poor financial planning has the tendency to lead to individual and corporate bankruptcy. This occurs when the person concerned in unable to meet up with cash and other personal/business obligations.

In crafting a financial plan, the following questions would require specific answers:

1. What objectives or goals do we intend to achieve?
2. How do we achieve these objectives?
3. What resources are required for the achievement of the identified objectives?
4. What monitoring, feedback and control mechanisms are we implementing to keep performance on track?

The Role of Vision in Financial Planning

A clear financial vision is the very first step for the development of a good financial plan. Vision is thus the foundation of financial planning. It is widely held that to think and feel beyond the present moment is an uncommon skill. What is common is the fact that lack of knowledge about the importance of clarity of financial vision is the common cause of failure in the management of individual and corporate finances.

Without vision, there are no standards. Where there no standards, there is nothing to measure performance against. Making profits or lack of it counts for nothing and the essence of managing personal finances is lost.

Clarity of financial vision and objectives provides a sense of:

1. Purpose
2. Mission
3. Performance Standards
4. Achievement or Lack of it

Vision provides the framework for detailed planning for the task ahead. Performance targets can then be set for income, expenditure, assets, liabilities and all the other elements of the financial plan. The financial plan is in effect the roadmap required to actualize the financial vision.

The Process of Financial Planning

Financial Planning may be seen as a process made up of the following steps:

Step 1: A clearly inspired view of the financial future.

Step 2: Definition of the financial goals and objectives.

Step 3: Strategy Identification

Step 4: Budgeting and Implementation

Step 5: Review and Control

For a financial plan to be realistic, the objectives of the plan must meet the SMART criteria. Objectives must be:

S—Specific

M—Measurable

A—Aligned to vision

R—Results-oriented

T—Time-scaled.

THE FINANCIAL VISION

The financial vision is usually expressed in a vision statement. The vision statement is to serve as a source of inspiration for future decision making. The vision statement is expected to provide a benchmark tool for detecting whether performance is in the line of sight or not. Because of this, the vision statement is often general although with some reasonable level of possibility in the achievement of some specific targets.

Describing a financial vision in a statement from the individual and corporate perspective is not an easy task. In a lot of instances, the initial vision statement will need to be continually refined as further insight and discussion take place on the subject matter.

For instance, a petrochemicals refining company may have the following as its vision statement: To become a dominant player in the downstream sector of the market by becoming the largest refiner and supplier of crude oil products.

The above example of a mission statement is both general (dominant player in the market) and specific (largest refiner and supplier of crude oil products).

Quite often, vision and mission are sometimes confused by most people. The difference is that while the vision statement is a statement of the future position that an individual attains to achieve, the mission statement communicates the vision by considering several factors. In essence, the mission statement is more specific and detailed than the vision statement.

THE FINANCIAL OBJECTIVE

Financial objectives need to clear, concrete, measurable and tangible for them to be meaningful. Financial objectives must not be abstract or general in nature. It is strongly recommended that financial objectives are made to meet the following criteria:

1. Specific—To be useful, financial objectives are required to be precise. Vague expressions of goals do no good as they deny the setting of standards for measuring achievement. The exactness of financial targets enables an individual or a company to know whether the targets have been achieved or not.
2. Measurability—In terms of size and scope. From the financial points of view, some measures of measurability that should be taken into consideration include cost of the desired outcome, the quality of desired outcome and the quantity of the desired outcome.

3. Alignment to Vision: Since the financial vision is the lens through which the entire activity of the individual or company is looked at, it is only natural that financial objectives are aligned to the vision of the entire undertaking. From the individual perspective, if someone has a vision of financial freedom for his family, his financial objective must align with the achievement of this vision. There is thus a need for goal congruence between both. Financial objectives are expected to contribute to the actualization of the financial vision.

4. Results-Oriented—The focus here is on the expected tangible outcome. Again, there is need for clarity on what the exact outcome of the financial objectives should be. This answers the question of what we intend to achieve with the financial objectives.

5. Time-scaled—This answers the question of when are we going to achieve the desired results? Without a timescale attached to the achievement of a particular financial milestone, it is impossible to say when success has been achieved. Due dates for the delivery of financial objectives have to be specific and clear.

Objectives are also very often confused with goals. Note that goals do not have measurements and thus non-specific. There are often expressed as general statements of direction. It is usual to have a general overriding financial goal either from the individual or corporate point of view. The specific details of those items that will now lead to the achievement of this goal may then be regarded as the objectives.

THE BUDGET AS A TOOL FOR FINANCIAL PLANNING AND CONTROL

The budget is a term that is commonly bandied about. But how many people are actually familiar with the concept of budgeting. In everyday usage of language, a lot of people associate budget with financial limitations. Once someone says; I am on a budget, it is implied that he or she has financial limitations. The practice is so common to the extent that people specifically go out to shop in budget shops and secure hotel accommodation at budget rates. The term budget has thus come to represent the word; cheap in everyday usage. Note that this is not the case or the intention with the financial budget.

The budget is an indispensable financial planning and control tool. The budget is the quantitative expression of financial plans for a future period. The quantitative expression means that the targets for the parameters are precise and time-bound. This enables the figures to serve as benchmark standards of cost, quality or quantity.

Financial Planning in the technical sense of the word may seem complex to most people. But the recommended rule is to keep your financial plans as simple as possible. The more complex a financial plan is, the less likely it will be achieved. Once performance targets are set for the key elements of the financial plan, the simple identification of the steps and procedures required to achieve these targets is deemed sufficient.

From the organizational point of view, the financial planning process which also includes budgeting is made up of the following steps:

Step 1: Identification of financial objectives

Step 2: Search for alternative courses of action

Step 3: Information gathering on the alternative courses of action

Step 4: Selection of alternative courses of action

Step 5: Implementation of the long term plan using annual budgets

Step 6: Monitoring of actual results

Step 7: Control mechanisms and budget modifications to keep performance on track.

Steps 5 to 7 represent the actual budget process. It therefore follows that the annual budget is an instrument of great significance to all organizations. The following represent some of the different types of budget that a corporate entity may prepare from time to time:

1. The long term budget
2. The annual budget
3. The cash budget
4. The production budget
5. The sales budget
6. The capital spending budget
7. The working capital needs budget
8. The human capital budget
9. The recurrent expenditure budget
10. The projects budget

An individual preparing a budget for personal use need not follow all the steps enumerated above. It is however important for everyone involved in making financial decisions to be clearly aware of the driving goals, quality targets as well as cost/time limitations for each financial undertaking.

Advantages of the Financial Budget

The budgetary system is thus an aid for the following:

1. The financial budget provides a formal planning framework for all future activities of the organization and the individual.
2. The budget also aids in the co-ordination of the various aspects of a business or a financial undertaking. A holistic view of the business

or personal objective necessitates the creation of a budget that incorporates the various aspects of a business or undertaking.

3. The approved financial budget of an organization is also a tool that implies management authorization of the principles, objectives and content of the financial budget.

4. The approved financial budget also to some extent serves as evidence of delegation of responsibilities. The identification of budget centers and budget owners in a budget document identifies who is responsible for what.

5. The specific quantitative measures expressed in the budget serve as performance standards. The standards form the basis for performance evaluation of the various budget centers. In addition, the budget can also be used to measure the performance of each budget owner. The budget owner is the person who has direct control over the achievement of the targets of a particular budget item or even budget centre.

6. The financial budget also serves as a tool for communicating and motivating people working in a group to achieve a common purpose. It can be used as a tool to focus attention and direct efforts towards the achievement of common goals.

7. Because reality is often different from the plan, the budget equally serves as a control tool. Having differences in actual performance from the budgeted performance is common. Investigating the causes of the differences prepares an organization to take corrective action required to keep the initial goal in focus.

The entire benefit of budgeting is lost when the budget control function is not implemented. Constant monitoring of performance and ensuring that current and future courses of action are in line with the desired objectives is a prerequisite. This does not however suggest that a financial budget should be a rigid document.

The importance of flexibility in Financial Budgeting

It is equally vital in crafting a financial plan that a relative degree of flexibility be introduced into the plan. The 'What If' scenario analysis is invaluable in this regard. The reason for this is that once one is locked rigidly into a plan, overachievement can equally pose the same risks and challenges as underachievement. The reality again is that is that it is difficult to find a situation whereby specific financial targets are accurately achieved. The rule is to identify a margin of success or failure within the range of financial targets.

Factors in the business environment change all the time, so the business environment is in constant flux. The same applies even to the personal environment of an individual. The rule is to always have a strong sense of awareness for what is strategically important in any given situation. To respond adequately to the dynamism of the business environment, budgets control mechanisms should be flexible and adaptable to changing scenarios.

Achieving your financial objectives must not be like solving a complex mathematical problem with a formula. You must design your approach to the objectives from various viewpoints. More often than not, factors that were considered less important at the planning stage become significant in the course of implementation. It is wise to take note as this reality impacts on financial strategy. Human factors also come into play. The implementation landscape is fluid and full of surprises. Most of all, it is instructive to keep your eyes on the ball and respond appropriately to the changing implementation landscape.

Our financial vision, objectives and budget should assist us in finding specific answers to the following questions:

- What is our primary goal?
- How to we intent to achieve this goal?

- What goods or services do we need to provide in order to achieve this goal?
- How much income or benefit can we generate from this course of action? (How? When? Where? In What Form?)
- What will it cost us (expenditure in terms of category, when, where?)
- How do we raise funds required to finance this undertaking?
- What assets must we acquire? (What Classes? How Much of Each Class? When to be acquired? From Where to acquire? How do we maintain the assets?)
- What about liabilities? (What liabilities to incur? When to incur? How much to incur? From whom to incur? What offset obligations? Whether cash or deferred payments or both?)

In summary, financial planning is an important key to success in the management of personal and corporate finances. Without it, success and failure mean the same thing. The vision helps to define the objectives. The budget represents the detailed quantitative expressions of these objectives.

CHAPTER SEVEN

LESSON THREE
JUSTIFICATION AND PRIORITISATION
OF EXPENDITURE

The Strategic Assessment Phase

Dealing with competing needs in the context of limited resources can only be effectively tackled through justification and prioritization. This step ensures that the so-called unlimited wants do not become a constraint to success in the management of finances.

Justification simply seeks a yes or no answer to expenditure decisions. To achieve financial goals and objectives, it often necessary to make certain expenditure decisions. The expenditure may be consumption or investment in nature.

The ultimate purpose of this justification is to determine whether in light of the income and asset targets that have been predetermined, it is necessary to incur expenditure in different scales and manner. Justification of expenditure should be premised on the critical importance of that expenditure to the achievement of desired income and asset targets.

Having justified all expenditure, the next step is to prioritize them. It does not matter whether the expenditure decision is consumption or investment natured. The key is to rank all expenditure in order of importance. This enables the identification of what and what should come first.

Once the scale of expenditure preference is drawn, expenditure decisions can then be organized in the context of limited financial resources. While justification answers questions of reasonableness and rightness of an expected expenditure, prioritization ranks those decisions in term of their contribution to our short term, medium term and long term contributions to achieving our financial objectives.

The Importance of Doing Cost/Benefit Analysis for Financial Decisions

The cost/benefit analysis is a technique commonly used in the public sector that involves the evaluation of say a financial expenditure proposal that does not have tangible results or where even the intention to make profit is not a driving objective.

However, it is equally important to apply similar techniques to a company's expenditure proposal. An individual may also consider the cost/benefit implications of choosing a particular financial investment option. The goal is not to assume that the management of personal finances must follow exactly the same pattern as that of corporate finances. But to inform that it is practically possible to apply similar financial principles for the justification of personal expenditure proposals.

After providing for his basic or physiological needs, an individual may have as a personal financial goal the intention to build a personal house, to develop a piece of commercial real estate or the setting up of a company to provide certain services. All these objectives require the sourcing and application of monies. These monies may be sourced from personal savings, personal assets, personal loans or even business loans.

As a rule, it is important to do a simple cost/benefit analysis of each major financial decision that is being proposed. If the benefits outweigh the cost, then the prospects of the decision is positive. But if the cost outweighs the benefit, it might be necessary to consider a rethink of the financial proposal. This practice does a whole lot of good to the individual as it helps to minimize the incidence of wasteful spending.

Dimensions of Cost

It is a known fact that when people hear about cost, they generally see cost from the purely monetary and quantitative points of view. This is quite misleading as the concept of cost goes beyond the monetary value. There are other dimensions of cost that should be considered when faced with decisions on money matters. They include:

1. Cost in terms of materials required
2. Cost in term of time
3. Cost in terms of labor
4. Cost in terms of other overheads
5. Cost in terms of experience and skill
6. The opportunity cost of a particular course of action
7. Cost in terms of reputation and honor

Some elements of cost are quite easy (such as materials, labor and overheads) to measure, quantify and assign monetary values to while others are difficult to assign monetary values to. If as an individual you know you cannot bear the full cost of a financial undertaking, it does not make sense to embark on such in the first place. Take proper note of all the direct and indirect elements of cost involved with a given financial decision and be certain you can accommodate such before you proceed with the expenditure plan.

Dimensions of Benefit

Just the way it is with cost, there are various dimensions of benefit accruable from a financial decision. Again a lot of people suffer from tunnel vision when it comes to assessing the potential benefits of a certain course of financial expenditure or action. People are prone to view benefits of a course of action only in monetary terms. Benefits may be:

1. Financial in nature such as the achievement of specific rate of return on investments, the attainment of a certain sales target, the achievement of the certain market growth rate, attainment of a specific level of profitability and so on.
2. Non-Financial in nature such as the benefit of becoming the dominant player in the market, the provider of the best quality product in the industry, business known for the best corporate social responsibility program and so on.

Prioritization facilitates the identification of areas of wasteful expenditure plans. The resulting expenditure scale of preference is thus streamlined by focusing on the most important and critical elements of the expenditure plan required for the achievement of financial objectives.

Financial objectives are the lens through which all expenditure plans are to be seen. Contribution to the achievement of the overall objective is the basis of importance and criticality. In preparing a personal financial scale of preference, the following tips should be borne in mind:

- Define clearly what your financial objectives are in the context of a given income or asset acquisition goal.
- Identify your limitations in terms of financial resources, time, skill and experience.
- Prepare a list of the expenditure decisions that is required to enable the achievement of the stated financial objectives.

- Analyze the expenditure decisions in detail and determine those that are consumption in nature and separate them from those that investment in nature.
- Justify the importance of those expenditure decisions in terms of need and reasonableness to the financial objective in focus.
- Rank in the order of importance in contribution to the overall financial objective.
- Match expenditure plans to the limiting constraints of financial resources, available time and expertise.
- Develop a realistic step by step plan of implementation.
- Follow through the implementation plan. Conduct regular reviews of performance and ensure that the acquired experience from reality continues to inform strategy going forward.
- Document the plans, fresh insights and lessons from experience for future reference.

CHAPTER EIGHT

LESSON FOUR
DEVELOP/ADOPT A FINANCIAL CODE
OF CONDUCT

The Action Phase

This is the active engagement phase of managing money. It is the stage at which strategy is expressed by action and where action also informs/impacts on strategy. A financial code of conduct is proposed for all so that individuals may act following a set of guiding principles or rules.

This is where the hands-on skill of practical financial management comes into play. It is the active engagement phase of the entire process. Due to the rigorous nature of this phase, there is a tendency amongst people to simply adopt a reactive mode to the entire process.

Most often at this stage, financial strategy seems to be suspended and people simply react to the signs and vibrations emanating from the immediate environment. First and foremost, it is vital to approach this phase with a strategic intent. The intention is to influence the eventual outcome of the financial transaction. Be it a negotiation, offer or acceptance situation or a bidding process.

Because thoughts are usually frozen once a process is set in motion, the suspended animation that ensues is often the root cause of the wide variations that result from interactions.

For instance, an individual desiring to acquire furniture visits a furniture shop. On each piece of furniture he notices a price tag. Without thinking any further he accepts the prices on these tags as the market value for those pieces of furniture. He goes back to his furniture purchase financial plan and attaches these values as the cost of furniture. He forgets the fact that the price of anything at any time is at best arbitrary. With some negotiation, he could have secured a better deal. Forget the fact that there is a price tag on each of the furniture items. The seller is there to sell, while the buyer is there to purchase. The striking price is usually the result of a consensus between the buyer and seller. In effect, the price tag is nothing but the asking price. A financially savvy customer/buyer will always negotiate because he is aware that a better deal usually comes from negotiation.

Income Conservatism and Expenditure Frugality

With respect to the management of personal finances, the guiding principle in relation to income and expenditure decisions are two-fold:

- With Income—Conservatism
- With Expenditure—Frugality

The principle of economy suggests that you strive to maximize benefit at the least cost. This applies to financial inflows as well as outflows. If income represents inflow, it is wise to be conservative about income expectations. It is pointless to have overstated income objectives since very often such income targets are unachievable. Income goals must be based on realistic premises and no harm comes from being conservative with personal income targets.

This does not however suggest that income targets should not be ambitious, but they should be challenging enough to warrant actions required for its achievement.

Frugality with all forms of expenditure is strongly advocated. This does not suggest that one should be miserly but to always act with a sense of economic consciousness. Expenditure represents outflows and caution is the watchword in this regard. The saying that people should open their wallets cautiously is relevant. Because once something goes out of the wallet, it does not come back in easily. A lot of effort is usually expended in the process. But come to think of it, it is actually easier to bring a dollar out of a wallet than to bring it back in. Don't you reason that there is some food for thought in this?

Frugality denotes some measure of prudence in the management of financial resources. Each dime should be spent with the future in mind. If it not worth spending in light of the desired future outcome, it is not worth spending at all. It therefore follows that the frugal mind is not only economical in the use of resources but also prudent in their application.

As outflows from net worth, consumption and investment expenditure all lead to reductions of disposable funds available to an individual, organization or society. To be frugal with expenditure requires discipline and foresight. Control over expenditure in a major success determining factor in personal and corporate financial management. No matter how much income an individual or a corporate entity generates, it would amount to nothing if there is lack of appropriate controls over expenditure.

It is customary for an assessment of the quality of financial decisions made to be done using the quality of expenditure decisions as a benchmark parameter. The outcome of expenditure decisions is in effect merely a reflection of the quality of financial decision making.

Frugal financial decision making involves some or all of the following:

- Establishment of clear expenditure goals.
- Prioritizing the goals and decisions required to achieve them.
- Calculating a near accurate estimate of the least cost of each course of expenditure action.
- Alignment of the available finance to expenditure needs.
- Implement based on the rule of thumb that guarantees maximum benefit at least cost.

In the context of the potential benefits derivable from an income point of view, frugality narrows down expenditure decisions to the most significant. This significance is measured in terms of financial budget usage, time allocation and manpower requirements.

Being frugal with expenditure enables an individual to keep expenditure plans straight and simple. The key assessment criteria are benefits and cost. It is considered wasteful to apply more resources to achieve a certain objective when it is practically possible to achieve same with less. What is usually needed is a bit of intuition, self restraint and a touch of discipline.

Thoughtful spending reinforces the culture of prudence and responsibility in the management of individual and corporate financial resources.

The Impact of Ethical Conduct on the Outcome of Financial Decisions

Individuals and companies do not exist in a vacuum. They are part and parcel of the larger society. Likewise, no modern society is self sufficient to the point that it does not transact with other societies. So financial decision making involves relationships between individuals, companies and societies.

Certain assumptions are held between parties involved in financial decision making. Though, these assumptions are what they mean it is useful to note that once these assumptions are threatened, the desired outcome of the related financial undertaking itself becomes uncertain. Some of the assumptions between two or more parties that are involved in financial transactions will include:

1. An assumption that both parties are acting in good faith to promote the mutual benefit of all that are involved in the process of creating wealth.
2. An assumption that the terms of a business or a financial transaction will be honored as at when due.
3. An assumption of integrity of the parties involved in a business or financial transaction.
4. An assumption of reliability in the currency of transaction. For instance, an assumption that the currency of business will remain acceptable as legal tender throughout the period of business transaction.
5. An assumption that the economic value of the currency of business will be relatively stable over the course of business. In other words, it is not anticipated that the currency will suffer significant loss in value during the course of transaction.
6. An assumption of faith in the legal and operational framework behind the business environment.

Because of the existence of these assumptions and many others, it is important that individuals who desire to succeed in the management of finances must be wary of their ethical conduct. Character is central to success in the management of money. Because success in this area is required on a continuing basis, the reputation of the individual in relation to money matters is critical to success. To be consistently successful in managing finances, people must have identified you with the following virtues:

1. Sincerity of Purpose
2. Reliability
3. Honesty and Integrity in Personal and Business Dealings

4. Fairness
5. Civility
6. Respect for Laws and Established Procedures
7. Strong ability for commercial negotiation
8. Effective business communication skills
9. Cautious optimism in the management of finances
10. General commercial wisdom

In contemplating a major financial undertaking, the individual must beware of the some of the aftereffects of financial decision making. After a major purchase, a buyer may feel buyers' remorse. If the purchase decision was not properly justified the situation is made worse and the experience becomes somewhat pathetic.

A Recommended Code of Conduct for Financial Dealings

For anyone who desires to succeed with the management of money, I recommend the following code of ethics. Successful money management is actually an unofficial field of specialization. Those who are successful at it know why while those who are unsuccessful do not know why.

I understand that a lot of people think that in money matters, one should be driven by pure self interest sometimes to the total exclusion of the interest of other parties. Well, understand that if the other parties also have this same view, then a win-lose situation becomes inevitable. The importance of this is that unless a business engagement is designed to promote the mutual benefit of the parties involved, then it is simply an exercise in futility. Sooner or later, the reality will become evident to all.

Just as is applicable in almost every professional discipline, the following fundamental code of ethics should be borne in mind by all those who desire to be successful in the practical management of money:

1. Financial Honesty and Integrity
2. Tact and Diplomacy in the handling of money matters
3. Fairness and Consideration for other parties involved in money transactions.
4. Due Skill and Diligence
5. Thorough Documentation and Records Keeping

While adequate planning and justifying of purchase decisions provide immense benefits, a good check to financial mismanagement is the adoption of the recommended code of ethics in the daily process of decision making. With the principles of income conservatism and expenditure frugality, it is highly unlikely that financial decision making will result in undesirable outcomes.

CHAPTER NINE

Lesson Five
Learning and Choosing Contentment

The Choice Phase

Regardless of the outcome of a financial decision, it is vital that the lesson inherent in an experience is not lost as this is vital to future financial strategy development. The more people learn from their failures, the less likely they will fail again.

Contentment is a choice and not a product of personal financial decision making. Individuals must understand that this choice is available to all and also have the courage to choose to have it. Contentment has a positive effect on future financial decision making for the decision maker.

Life is a journey and not a destination. Life is a challenge and not a barrier. Once the first breadth is taken, everything else becomes experience and then history. How do you become more aware of your environment and the people that inhabit it? How do you acquire more skill and competence in dealing with the situations that life is bound to throw at you? These are questions that constantly beg for answers.

Like a wheel in motion, the chain of experiences that inform our knowledge continues to turn. As we acquire more knowledge over time, we are expected to be better equipped with the tools that will guarantee long term survival, prosperity and stability in all our dealings. This simple truth affects the financial and non-financial aspects of our lives.

Learning involves acquiring knowledge through careful study of various phenomena. This could come from direct observations, personal experiences and learning from the experiences of others. A good learner usually maintains an open mind. The open mind is thus a fertile field for the implantation of brand new ideas.

An average individual looks at past financial experience from a negative point of view. People will acknowledge to having had a bruising financial experience. But the flip side of the argument is that, perhaps if you had not lost 1,000 Dollars five years ago you would have lost 100,000 Dollars today!

The message is simple; in the outcome of every financial undertaking there is a key lesson for the vigilant student. It is a known fact that people lose more from success than they gain by failure. Failure reinforces the need to acquire more expertise on the subject matter so it encourages perfection.

If there is any area of life where perfection is desired, it is in the management of personal and corporate finances. Every lesson and every experience counts so that the same mistakes are not repeated going forward.

Research has consistently shown that regardless of your pedigree, financial position, age or status in society every human being is bound to experience a unique form of challenges in the very many aspects of life. The problem for most people lie with the way they deal with the challenges when they come.

Learning from our own financial experience is the foundation of our unique preparation for future challenges. The challenges will come whether we want them or not. But we must be ready to deal properly with them at the right time. Failure to learn from our own personal experiences is akin to failure to acknowledge that we exist for a purpose.

Following the crash of financial markets in 2007/2008 and the resulting specter of economic challenges in most advanced societies, there is a growing interest to focus attention on measures that will promote happiness and contentment. It was observed that financial success or lack of it cannot guarantee happiness for the majority of the world's population.

Anthony Robbins in his book titled; **Awaken the Giant Within** regards emotional destiny as the only true success. It is a proven fact that for over the three thousand (3,000) strands of emotions that the human race is yet to fully describe, we only experience an average of about a dozen per week. The emotions of happiness, anger, sadness, despair, joy, excitement, fulfillment, disappointment, pride and others tend to rank high on the regular experience scale. This is because they represent the range of emotions that most people are acutely familiar with.

Emotional Intelligence studies cover the effect of positive and negative emotions on human thought and behavior. The positive emotions such as love, happiness, joy and excitement have a calming effect on most people. It was argued that while we cannot deny experiencing negative emotions such as anger, frustration and disgust we must recognize such emotions and take steps that will neutralize the negative impacts of feeling such emotions.

Terms like the emotional brain, the emotional mind, the emotional heart and the emotional body have become serious subjects of academic and practical enquiry. The field of Happiness Economics is on the horizon and a lot of debate is currently on this subject matter.

Mastering your emotions is the platform for all success. My position is that contentment is a choice that is freely available to all. Regardless of the outcome of your past financial decision, you must have the wisdom and willpower to CHOOSE emotional contentment.

I would define a life of success as a life of quality in all the key areas of life. These include the emotional, the physical as well as the spiritual aspects of life. A life of quality is a life of deep contentment, happiness and tranquility. A life of quality is a life that is in perfect peace and in perfect harmony with nature and its elements. Living such a worthy life is actually a CHIOCE that is available to all.

Steps to the Mastery of Emotions

To improve the outcomes of financial decision making, the following steps are recommended for the mastery of emotions:

1. Step One: Know the difference between positive and negative emotions.
2. Step Two: In each situation, clearly identify the type of emotion you are feeling.
3. Step Three: Find out the root cause of the emotion you are feeling at the time.
4. Step Four: If it is a positive emotion, understand that the emotion is there to empower you. If it is a negative emotion, take note.
5. Step Five: Take concrete measures to mitigate the escalation of the negative emotion.
6. Step Six: Learn the lessons inherent in the financial experience you have just had.

Personal Character Attributes for Success in the Management of Money/Finances

In summary, the individual who desires to be successful in the management of money/finances must cultivate and imbibe the following as character attributes:

1. A keen sense of commercial and business awareness
2. Openness and willingness to always learn
3. Self Knowledge
4. Mastery of Time
5. Mastery of Emotions
6. Maintain Good Interpersonal Relationships
7. Courage
8. Cautious optimism
9. Self Confident
10. Maintain a can-do attitude

A common mistake nowadays is the measurement of success purely based on financial or material achievements. It is in fact a short-sighted and misleading approach to the measurement of success. Since no two individuals begin life at the same level financially, it is misleading to use a financial yardstick as the basis of their success in life. What about other factors like impact on other people?

It is common knowledge that there are so many people who are financially rich yet extremely unhappy. How do you then explain such a phenomena. Financial achievement is not the only factor that leads to happiness and contentment. In fact experience has shown that sometimes and for some individuals, financial success can lead to further discontentment. The message here is simple, regardless of what happens people should always choose contentment and happiness over the negative emotions that come with some experiences. This way healthy living is promoted to the benefit of the individual, the family and the society in general.

A Practical 10-Step Guide

1. Step 1: Clearly imagine what your financial future would be like.

2. Step 2: Identify the things you need to do to get there.

3. Step 3: Determine what changes in your personal attributes, attitudes and investments that are required for the attainment of your future financial vision.

4. Identify all your sources of income.

5. Estimate what is expected from each source. Be realistic and conservative about these estimates.

6. Identify all your expenditure needs. Isolate consumption expenditure needs from investments expenditure needs.

7. Based on your total finances available for investment growth purposes, prioritize your investment expenditure based on their cost and benefit potentials.

8. Allocate and apportion your funds for maximum benefits.

9. Control, monitor and review the outcomes of your financial decisions. Ensure corrective measures are taken to keep performance on track.

10. Always learn from each experience and choose emotional contentment.

Throughout the above process, take note that in your interactions with people you will need to reflect the key character attributes required for success in the management of finances.

CONCLUSION

Since emotional success is a choice, it therefore follows that success in the management of personal and corporate finances is equally a choice that we are all free to make.

The connection between financial achievement and individual happiness or contentment is an interesting area of academic as well as professional research. Modern man, completely sold on the idealistic supremacy of financial achievement has soon come to realize that true success goes beyond the financials. How much good does it do a man to have all the financial resources he can ever dream about and yet have the vast majority of people living in penury?

We all know that the emotions behind money matters are strong. They are compelling and very often intriguing. It is quite an uncommon skill to master the art of managing finances. Financial mastery ensures that at all times there is a very clear financial vision of what is desired as well as the development of the strategies required for the achievement of those objectives.

It is normal to experience the pressure of everyday living. It is equally normal to experience financial pressure from time to time as we do not have absolute control over all the factors that affect our finances. It is however misleading to assume that with more financial resources at our disposal, the pressure would simply disappear. Very often, the accumulation of more financial resources leads to an increase in the pressure to either spend or find creative ways of safeguarding the resource base.

The push for greater accumulation of financial resources if left unchecked becomes a life-long challenge for most people. It is wise to periodically take the heat off and reassure oneself that success in the management of personal finances is not all about the money.

Life, Liberty, Freedom and happiness are all desirable. A life of liberty is a life of freedom. Freedom to chose and act in a way that is beneficial to the individual and the larger society. A life of freedom of choice is invariably a life that can lead to happiness. The choice lies in the hands of the individual concerned. Just the way you are the only that can determine what you do with your time and your mind, you are the only that can determine what you allow yourself to feel at any point in time. The choice is yours.

NOTES

1. Allen, Robert G. Multiple Streams of Income: *How to Generate a Lifetime of Unlimited Wealth.* New Jersey: John Wiley & Sons, Inc, 2005.

2. Covey, Stephen R. *The 7 Habits of Highly Effective People.* New York: Simon and Schuster, 1998.

3. Gimian, James and Barry Boyce. *The Rules of Victory: How to Transform Chaos and Conflict.* Boston and London: Shambhala Publications, 2008.

4. Handy, Charles. *The Age of Unreason.* Harvard Business School Press, 1991.

5. Hill, Napoleon. *Napoleon Hill's Keys to Success: the 17 Principles of Personal Achievement.* New York. Dutton. 1994.

6. Greene, Robert and Joost Elffers. *The 48 Laws of Power.* New York: Viking, 1998.

7. Greene, Robert and Joost Elffers. *The Art of Seduction.*

8. Greene, Robert and Joost Elffers. *The 33 Strategies of War.*

9. Kepes, Gyorgy. Language of Vision. Chicago: Paul Theobald. 1944

10. Kiyosaki, Robert. *Rich Dad Poor Dad.* New York: Warner Books. 1997.

11. Lakein, Alan. *How to Get Control of your Time and Your Life.* New American Library, 1996.

12. Maxwell, John C. *The 21 Irrefutable Laws of Leadership: Follow them and People will Follow You.* Nashville: Thomas Edison Publishers, 1998.

13. Nash, Susan. *Becoming a Consultant: How to Start and Run a Profitable Consulting Business.* Plymouth: How to Books, 1999.

14. Noonan, David. *Aesop and the CEO: Powerful Business Insights from Aesop's Ancient Fables.* Nashville: Thomas Nelson Inc., 2005.

15. Robbins, Anthony. *Awaken the Giant Within: How to take Immediate Control of your Mental, Emotional, Physical and Financial Destiny!* New York: Simon and Schuster New York, 1991.

16. Study Text, ACCA Paper 3.5. *Strategic Business Planning and Development.* London: BPP Professional Education, 2003.

17. Textbook, ACCA Paper 2.4: Financial Management and Control. Middlesex: Foulks Lynch Publications, 2002.

18. Textbook, ACCA Paper 2.6: Audit and Internal Review. Middlesex: Foulks Lynch Publications, 2003.

19. Tracy, Brian. *Maximum Achievement: Strategies and Skills That Will Unlock Your Hidden Powers to Succeed.* Benin City: Beulahland Publications, 1993.

20. Trump, Donald. *The Art of the Deal.* New York: Random House, 1988.

SOME PUBLISHED ARTICLES
OF THE AUTHOR

1. The North Atlantic Debt Crisis: Lessons for Emerging and Developing Countries
2. Liquidity versus Profitability: The Dilemma of the Finance Manager
3. The Global Economic Crisis and the Challenge of Reforming Banking and Finance Practice.
4. The Icarus Paradox: Why some Nigerian Banks Failed
5. The Timeless Value of Emotional Intelligence
6. Nigeria's Sovereign Wealth Fund: Prospects and Tips for Getting it Right
7. Potentials of the Nigerian Sovereign Wealth Fund
8. Nigeria's Sovereign Wealth Fund: Avoiding the Pitfalls of Implementation
9. The IMF Article IV Consultation Report on Nigeria: Analysis and Implication
10. The Need for a Common Financial Accounting and Financial Reporting Framework for Nigerian Banks

ABOUT THE AUTHOR

Mr. Shafii Ndanusa is a chartered accountant with memberships of the Association of Chartered Certified Accountants (ACCA, United Kingdom) and the Institute of Chartered Accountants of Nigeria (ACA; ICAN Nigeria). He holds the Master Financial Professional (MFP) charter of the American Academy of Financial Management (AAFM, USA) and is also a Fellow of the American Academy of Financial Management (FAAFM, USA). He received his Bachelor of Science degree in Accounting from the University of Abuja in Nigeria and his MBA from the Ahmadu Bello University Zaria Nigeria. He is an acknowledged expert in enterprise financial management, wealth management, strategy development, business/economic research, statistical analysis and treasury management. He currently has over fifteen years of work experience cutting across a wide range of corporate finance and administration functions. He has authored over fifteen (15) papers that have been widely published. His areas of general research interest include public finance/accounting, financial management, banking, economic policy/strategy, wealth/asset management, business strategy and enterprise resource planning. He lives in Abuja, Nigeria.